You're key to financial freedom.

A simple way to financial success.

Find out how other people get rich.

Table of contents:

"Coach personal growth":
Oleg Kolpakov.

DESCRIPTION:

INTRODUCTION:

LEVELS OF FINANCIAL PROTECTION:

CONSIDER THE LEVEL OF FINANCIAL FREEDOM:

HOW TO ACHIEVE NEW RESULTS:

OBSTACLE ON THE PATH TO SUCCESS:

WHERE DO MONEY:

BELIEVE IN YOURSELF:

EMOTIONAL INTELLIGENCE:

RAISING REVENUES:

FORMULA OF WEALTH:

INCOME SEGMENTS:

"Coach personal growth":
Oleg Kolpakov.

COST REDUCTION:

INVESTMENTS:

PERSONAL FINANCIAL PLAN:

Conclusion:

ENTRY:

Do you want to know how successful people have gained financial independence?

You wonder what this know what rich don't know you?

Make money know how many. This teaches us universities and books.

Not everyone who earns well can be called financially free because making money is only part of the success.

The main thing you need to know how to increase and dispose of them properly.

"Coach personal growth":
Oleg Kolpakov.

Knowledge about this owns a narrow circle of people, and really working information publicly available is very small.

If you want to learn this secret and gain financial freedom, then this book will help you succeed!

Thanks to this book, you gain access to knowledge, which will bring you to begin to live as you want and not think more about the lack of funds!

"Coach personal growth":
Oleg Kolpakov.

DESCRIPTION:

What you will learn and learn by reading the book:

The primary importance of proper placement goals, vision for their lives and understanding why you live.

How to draw up a tentative plan of action and put the task to pass certain stages of development.

How to properly invest and get rid of unnecessary and superfluous spending.

"Coach personal growth":
Oleg Kolpakov.

How to pick the right investment strategy and avoid big mistakes.

Examples of stories of real people, past the road to financial freedom.

How to act in critical situations involving money.

Situations of life, that's familiar to everyone:

Want to buy yourself something you want and you have to take out loans or tell yourself, then at other times.

When your income increases, and costs begin to rise, too.

Go to favorite work just to earn money.

Take new loans, loans and think, how then to pay debts.

See how other people earn more, work less and you live as they want.

You read a lot of different books, how to become a financially

"Coach personal growth":
Oleg Kolpakov.

independent man, but nothing changes in your life.

 You can list much more generally limits in your life is missing.

MEANS this book is for you!

INTRODUCTION:

Hello, dear reader!

 Thank you that you have the time and attention to the reading of this book. My book was created in order for you to receive your benefit.

All information here is me and verified by experience.

There was a time when I myself faced a financial crisis and got out of it with this knowledge I gathered in this book.

"Coach personal growth":
Oleg Kolpakov.

This knowledge helped me gain financial independence and freedom, now I am implementing your lifestyle, your goals, and dreams.

The book tells you about how to achieve financial well-being and realize their dreams.

Let's get started!

"Coach personal growth":
Oleg Kolpakov.

Find out what your goals are:

Financial freedom is one of the levels of financial protection and this level is measured by a specific amount of money.

To make the first step to financial freedom, you need to get to decide what you want and what is for you financial freedom!

"Coach personal growth":
Oleg Kolpakov.

LEVELS OF FINANCIAL PROTECTION:

1) Financial Security Reserve money, which will suffice you to six months of life without working.

When you are insured from what money you won't be if you lose your job

Financial security is the amount of savings equal to six current spending.

"Coach personal growth":
Oleg Kolpakov.

Calculate this parameter: multiply your average monthly expenses for six and you get the amount that you will refer to financial security.

2) A financial independence an opportunity not to depend on money does not depend on income from active income earned from such proceeds that have to do with their hands and head.

You can still say that financial independence is such an amount of money, which is enough for ensuring their standard of living,

i.e. ensuring costs don't matter
What're you are not.

This financial independence gives
passive income.

Passive income that you receive,
regardless of whether or not you
are working.

  For example, you've got to rent
an apartment or get interested
from a bank deposit.

  Similarly, financial independence
is a capital (money), which lies in

the Bank on the account under 9% per annum and interest covers your minimum monthly consumption.

Calculate the level of financial independence, may be knowing the amount of your 150 minimum cost!

3) Financial freedom.

Multiply 150 on the desired income, i.e. desired level of costs and you get capital to financial freedom.

Financial freedom as well as financial independence and financial security, measured in money, in a specific amount of money.

What to do now with all these levels? Moving on!

CONSIDER THE LEVEL OF FINANCIAL FREEDOM:

What is your desired income?

How much do you want to have an income?

And here begins to rise.

Now run a small rendering that will help determine what you specifically want.

Now imagine a future when you already have everything you now only want.

"Coach personal growth":
Oleg Kolpakov.

At this future time, your dreams and ideas are executed.

Imagine that it has been 6-8 years in your future, then ask yourself the following questions:

What happened during this time?

What happened?

What do you have?

"Coach personal growth":
Oleg Kolpakov.

What you have now is in the future?

What do you do, what kind of lifestyle do?

Who you are?

The main thing is that you have purchased, here's the thing that I wanted to have money, what is it? Look for more info.

That implemented?

What dreams, ideas, goals?

"Coach personal growth":
Oleg Kolpakov.

What to itself did not deny!

And now you want to go back to reunions' and analyze that entire saw it.

Write down everything that you will have in the future that you already realized what goals, dreams, lifestyle, that came true.

Your task: write a list of what you saw.

"Coach personal growth":
Oleg Kolpakov.

Everything you want to accomplish through these 6-8 years.

Recorded?

Now look what you have written there, just whether or not enough?

And now count how much money all this need right now?

Record the data on the contrary your desires and calculate the Grand total.

Further, the total fixed amount of monthly acquisition and "needs" multiply by 150 your minimum cost!

Get a grand total.

This will be the most capital, the amount of money that will allow you to realize all your financial plans.

This is the cost of dreams.

"Coach personal growth":
Oleg Kolpakov.

Take a look at the amount of money that turned out to be.

The real figure? Is this money actually real?

In early may or may not believe. But at the same time. We understand that the amount relatively real. Regarding tomorrow or concerning someone else, but, nevertheless, it's real money!

Take a look at that kind of money will surely be disposed of by someone from your surroundings.

"Coach personal growth":
Oleg Kolpakov.

You probably know these people who have that kind of money to eat!

So, it's absolutely real!

Now it remains a very important question-how making this reality for yourself?!

HOW TO ACHIEVE NEW RESULTS:

What we have now is the money that we are now somehow earning.

This is the structure of our income, the amount of our income, expenses; it is also the result of our work, right?

Let's call it "result 1"

And what we want in the future, it is also the result and calls it "Result2.

In order to get any result, you need to do something, to act.

These actions differ: "action 2" is opposed to "activity1.

What we're doing now is "action 1" and leads us to the "Platform1".

And expect that if we do the same thing every day, will there be any other result.

To reach "result 2" must do "action 2". True?

"Coach personal growth":
Oleg Kolpakov.

It seems that everything is very simple; you just need to do "action 2".

But constantly something interferes? As if something stops different obstacles!?

Even if we do "action 2"-we still return back to the

"Action 1» and we continue to do the same thing again!

"Coach personal growth":
Oleg Kolpakov.

What makes us do such actions? These are our Thoughts!

Have you noticed that people who have "**result 2**", have any other thoughts in your head and they somehow think differently, even speak!

If talking with these people, then you will not understand them. The level of thinking to another.

You've probably read smart books on positive thinking, to get "**result 2**"? And noticed that on the next

"Coach personal growth":
Oleg Kolpakov.

day after reading even the thought already!

But then you back returns to the previous thoughts!

Why is this happening?

Now remind yourself 5-7 years ago and tell me what kind of results have you had the same as now?

Probably similar to the same zone "1" and "2"?

"Coach personal growth":
Oleg Kolpakov.

The important thing is that the transition from the "1 result «in "result 2" occurred, or on the contrary, everything remained at the same level?

That you moved forward? Time? Right, this is the goal!

Everything that you move forward from one result to the next and better results, it is always the goal!

If you now look at people who are 5-7 years ago were in the first link, you'll see that some remained there as well!

Why is it so? Just they didn't have goals! Dreams and desires and goals were not!

The goal that is the only reason that you are moving forward.

The dream is useful, but only in order to create the dreams of goal!

What really you will move forward this goal!

"Coach personal growth":
Oleg Kolpakov.

But sometimes you will be something interfering!

What is it?

OBSTACLE ON THE PATH TO SUCCESS:

You decide what are the purposes of dreams, now you have a list that you can move forward.

Despite the fact that your objectives can be wonderful, you still remain the most interesting action level.

"Coach personal growth":
Oleg Kolpakov.

When we know what we have to do this very badly want to have a purpose.

And that we may prevent? What prevents us from realizing big money are dreams, to be who I want? What is it?

1) Laziness: when you postpone important things for later.

2) Fear: When are you afraid that something will not work or you do not will understand everything? Think others might, but I can't.

"Coach personal growth":
Oleg Kolpakov.

3) Uncertainty: your doubts, a lot of you seem not feasible. Constantly say I do not know how, etc.

Here they are the main obstacles on the road to success!

WHERE DO MONEY:

Money is a universal medium of Exchange.

"Coach personal growth":
Oleg Kolpakov.

Money comes in different forms: paper, coins, in gold, in electronic form.

Some people have more money, and others less.

If money is a universal medium of Exchange, it means that the money of the people, they have something to them came, agree?

Question: what came to them money?

For work? Means in order to have more money, need more work?

Mean billionaires work in more

"Coach personal growth":
Oleg Kolpakov.

than you? No!

 Billionaires just invented something, they are more work!

Here is what is the difference between the rich from the poor people who have what the missing brains.

 If drain only enough for a simple job and salary, respectively.

If you have enough brains to come up with something more serious: the Organization, something useful for people that value, then the money will come more.

 It follows from this that the

generator of money you have in your head and you get exactly as much money as you have enough brains.

Your brains to determine how much you're worth.

Hence, to have more money to receive more need to do something on the brain and head.

Need to change something in your head first.

First, you need to turn on your head, where the main switch, which leads you to money?

FAITH IN YOURSELF!

"Coach personal growth":
Oleg Kolpakov.

BELIEVE IN YOURSELF:

The first switch that to you decides to jump from one amount of money different is your belief in yourself!

Big money does not reach you because you just do not believe in the possibility of that money for them.

"Coach personal growth":
Oleg Kolpakov.

First of all, you need to do away with this question:

"can I?"

EMOTIONAL INTELLIGENCE:

Scientists, research, found no direct correlation between IQ and a degree of success!

If not IQ, what determines the

result and success?

What then determines the level of success where he comes from?

Scientists have brought another factor: parameter, which was called "emotional intelligence"

Scientists saw this feature as "knowledge is not to determine the outcome"

Why is it so that I know what to do, but don't, why?

Because there are internal obstacles: laziness, fear, uncertainty, and so on.

Of course, when there is objective, it itself is inspiring, but what about when you really need to do something, and you're still not doing?

As you guess, you need to do in order to get closer to your goals and dreams, but something makes you continue to sit in one place!

Emotional intelligence, it's just the same feature that the emotions rather than the intellect, how much emotion, ability to manage themselves, take decisions, Act!

"Coach personal growth":
Oleg Kolpakov.

Emotional intelligence consists of:

1. The ability to control their emotions.

2. Ability to make a decision, despite the lack of information.

3. Confidence, as the internal state.

4. Keeping fear under the control of the mind.

When we start doing something new, interesting, we are faced with the fact that we are afraid to continue.

"Coach personal growth":
Oleg Kolpakov.

As this condition keeps under control?

You need to act, despite the fact that scary!

This is what is called emotional intelligence, which allows you to operate and manage their condition.

Emotional intelligence can be trained, as well as IQ.

For example, in training.

How can you learn to manage your fear?

"Coach personal growth":
Oleg Kolpakov.

When you pass through a State of fear. Include an internal conversation "I can!"

Even just words the right words the words "I can!", attached to the force of action!

Say these words as often as possible!

Your wealth starts with that!

And then it's simple!

RAISING REVENUES:

Have you noticed that the higher the income, the greater the costs?

If we simply raise revenue without having to make it all not spend, we have little left.

That is, we increase revenue and costs are rising, too.

For example a year ago, you thought that I would be earning a certain amount and start delay.

Here you already earn wanted, but capital why not delayed? What's the matter?

Case in the formula for which you are applying for your money.

"Coach personal growth":
Oleg Kolpakov.

And what I'll introduce to you now is a formula of wealth!

FORMULA OF WEALTH:

The fact of the matter is that when you earn and spend everything you earn is a formula of poverty!

And no matter how much you earn, if you have nothing, you still are in poverty formula.

With this approach, you do not

form your capital!

If you have a capital formed and constantly growing you always have and will be on the money.

Now, the main thing is to begin to follow the formula of wealth.

What is the formula for wealth?

1) Earn: so somehow create money, create a business get with its income, invest-get some dividends.

Go to work or find work, most importantly earn create money!

2) Accumulate: Spending is not all that is earned, and then delayed.

3) Multiply: the amount of money that you have postponed, you need to multiply, further squeeze money from this.

Earn + gain + multiply = wealth formula!

95% of rich people, who have the status of more than one million dollars, earned his fortune just such a formula.

The first formula-earn.

How can you do it?

 Where may you have sources of income?

INCOME SEGMENTS:

There are 6 segments of income:

1), customary for many people a means of earning.

2) To itself work, perform the work, provide different services.

3) Business, one of the possible sources of income.

4) Invest when you work your money when you invest your money.

"Coach personal growth":
Oleg Kolpakov.

5) The social segment, students receives a stipend, pensioners receive a pension, the disabled receive benefits, in this segment, you can use and many other opportunities for receipt of income.

6) Gifts, this includes Lottery and inheritance and finds treasures or when grant money, it is also a source of income.

For all of these 6 segments has its own strategy, because each can make big money.

"Coach personal growth":
Oleg Kolpakov.

Just in every segment of the money are made differently, using different strategies.

COST REDUCTION:

I do not want to and not easy to do. The great temptation to spend more when incomes rise.

But, if you decide to follow the formula of wealth, then, after increasing incomes, your main task is to reduce costs and keep costs from rising.

How can we reduce costs? To manage costs!

"Coach personal growth":
Oleg Kolpakov.

Basic rules to reduce costs:

1) Delay of no less than 10% of the income of all income.

   It is recommended to defer 50%, but start to defer such income amount at once will be difficult, and you can go to this gradually, leaving no less than 10%.

   If for you, it would be difficult to hold off the first time, you can start with 3%, increasing to 5%.

2) Keep a strict accounting of expenses.

   Proven observations and

statisticians that when conducting a strict accounting of expenses there has been a reduction in the cost of 10-15%. Check for yourself!

3) Plan your budget and stick to it. When you plan your spending, you manage your money and raise the probability of hitting your budget and avoid unnecessary, unreasonable expenses.

4) Save up bonuses:

Now a lot of loyalty programs that enable you to accumulate bonuses for purchases.

Earn bonuses for their regular purchases and money spent will bring additional benefits.

  Spending money differently, you can accumulate extra bonuses and save on future purchases.

5) Save:

  Looking for new ways to buy cheap, meaning not the cheap stuff, and not to overpay extra money for what you buy.

  For example, use discount cards to buy on sales, use the Internet-shops and in other ways, giving the opportunity to buy the same thing but cheaper!

Why don't we want to delay?

We think that this 10% pending, it is a trifle.

But this trifle, one year turns into in a decent amount.

If 10-year delays, such a little thing can turn into millions!

INVESTMENTS:

If those savings, invest, and invest, then eventually it will turn out good annual rate, at which it is already possible to live well.

You need to plan and prepare various strategies, how to invest their money with big interest.

Opportunities multiply money:

1) Bank.

The Bank, this is a great opportunity with a guarantee, multiply your money.

The Bank gives some decent interest.

2) Real estate.

The apartment, which you can buy at a low price and then sell it to the repair.

You can and take an apartment or Office for rent.

3) Shares.
The action will allow you to quickly multiply your money.
But here, too, need to know the strategy.

4) Mutual funds.

"Coach personal growth":
Oleg Kolpakov.

If you do not want to risk them or understand the investments, there are mutual funds, in which specialists are engaged in.

Mutual funds are one of the types of fiduciary management when you do not want to understand the intricacies and trust professionals

Professionals take your money in the Office and take no great reward, and the rest give you.

5) Business.

Business, when what is bought and sold, or provided services.

"Coach personal growth":
Oleg Kolpakov.

The business also provides an opportunity for multiplication of money.

6) Precious metals. You can make good money in a crisis. A very profitable way.

7) Forex is a currency market, playing on the difference in exchange rates.

Need knowledge and strategy. You can examine and quickly multiply your money.

8) Attachments:

The most profitable type of

investment, investment in yourself.

Its seminars, training, receiving special education, information, it can all turn into money, even larger dividends.

Creating their image and brand. Your name will always brand.
What is the brand?

The brand is a specific Association, a certain attitude, a certain description of you.

It is not important to you, go to work, or are engaged in private practice, business, public

"Coach personal growth":
Oleg Kolpakov.

activities, your name will always be something to indicate.

You always put in your name!

Now let us remember all the steps to financial freedom:

1) Define objectives. The main first step, but if it is not done, then further steps would not be feasible.

2) Believe in them. Believe that this is all possible, probably for you, and move in before.

3) Raise their incomes. Use strategy to increase revenue. If

the income is not increased, then your rate is not rising.

4) Reduce their expenses. If income increases, the need to reduce costs.

5) Invest. Each of these steps is really a step toward financial freedom.

Important if any step is not taken, the likelihood that you won't reach the end!

As all combine? With the help of a personal financial plan!

"Coach personal growth":
Oleg Kolpakov.

PERSONAL FINANCIAL PLAN:

A personal financial plan is a plan that combines your income, expenses, and financial goals.

The personal financial plan differs from that of the budget because the notion there is only budget revenue and expenditure.

In a personal financial plan, in addition to the budget, have your financial goals and investment component of the plan.

"Coach personal growth":
Oleg Kolpakov.

If you have your own personal financial plan you have and map that identifies where to move.

You know, how should you want to increase your income and the level at which you want to keep spending.

Financial plan this is a very powerful and motivating tool. Make your financial plan and stick to it!

One question appears HOW IT IMPLEMENT?

A new piece of knowledge, another book, another dollop of

discoveries. It's time to translate all of this from the knowledge-experience!

The best way to turn knowledge into skills is training.

   Training is special tools that transform your knowledge into skills!

What needs to be done to consolidate and strengthen the knowledge in this Book?

   1) Play the game "by Robert Kiyosaki Cashflow 101 and 202".

 In this game, you will be able to pass wealth formula in real time.

Find where to play in your city, or buy yourself this useful game.

 2) Take a course or training on managing personal finances, "which teach you proper handling with money.

 3) Start from today, to apply all this knowledge!

 After studying this book, you will have the opportunity to realize their dreams, goals, and objectives!

"Coach personal growth":
Oleg Kolpakov.

Conclusion:

Dear reader, I want you to thank for your attention and your time.

Thank you that you have read this book through.

I hope yours has been helpful information you have read. Follow all these rules, on the road to financial freedom.

All these rules, I will respect every day and get your results previously only dreamed of.

I wish you find in future financial

"Coach personal growth":
Oleg Kolpakov.

independence. Success and achievements in your life.

All you good!

With respect to you:

"Coach, personal growth": Oleg Kolpakov.

"Coach personal growth":
Oleg Kolpakov.